Gravity

Contents

Dan Greenberg

Why do things that go up come back down?

The answer is gravity.
Gravity is an invisible force.

The girl jumps up.
Gravity pulls her down to the ground.

What things are pulled by gravity?

Everything on Earth is pulled by gravity. Gravity pulls the leaves down. Gravity even pulls the water down from a waterfall.

When birds fly,
the Earth's gravity
still pulls on them.
Gravity keeps them
from flying too
far away from the
Earth.

Is gravity always working?

On or near the Earth, gravity is always at work.
It is at work when things are falling.
It is at work when things are sitting still.

When the box is turned over, gravity sends the blocks tumbling to the ground.

But when the blocks are stacked, gravity holds them in place.

Without gravity, even a tiny puff of wind would make the girl and her blocks float up in the air.

Is there gravity in space?

Even the moon is pulled by gravity. The Earth's gravity keeps the moon from floating away in space.

The pull is not strong enough, however, to bring the moon down to the Earth. But it keeps the moon in place circling around the Earth.

Spaceships can take people far from the Earth.

During a space mission, these astronauts use special straps to hold themselves and their tools in place.

When they are that far away, the pull of the Earth's gravity has little effect on people. Far from the Earth, people and things in a spaceship float.

When the spaceship moves closer to the Earth, the pull of the Earth's gravity becomes stronger. When they return to Earth, the astronauts no longer float.

Here on Earth, every person and thing is pulled by gravity. The batter can bat the ball and send it flying . . .

but sooner or later, it will come back down!